# Au Sable River

# Au Sable River

Bob Linsenman

*Frank* **Amato**
PORTLAND

# River Journal

## Volume 5, Number 3, 1998

### Dedication

For Carl and for Marc—my father, my son.

### About the Author

Bob Linsenman has been fly fishing (exclusively) for more than 40 years. He fishes throughout North America and the Caribbean, but his favorite and home water is Michigan's Au Sable River.

He is a fly-fishing guide and writer. His published books are *Michigan Trout Streams: A Fly Angler's Guide* and *Great Lakes Steelhead: A Guided Tour for Fly Anglers,* W. W. Norton, (Both with Steve Nevala). His articles appear in *Fly Fisherman, The Fly Fisher, American Angler, Midwest Fly Fishing,* and *Wild Steelhead & Salmon.* He is the editor of the *Riverwatch,* the journal of The Anglers of the Au Sable.

Bob's daughter Cireé lives in New Mexico and his son Marc resides in Chicago. He owns two old 4WD Chevy trucks, 21 fly rods, one drift boat, three shotguns, and a good camera. Bob lives with two labrador retrievers in a cabin near the Au Sable. He is obviously single.

◆

## Acknowledgments

A pledge of gratitude and service to all those who have been helpful through the years. Specific thanks for assisting with this project go to the late Hugh Beaman, to Miles Chance, Doug Elbinger, JoAnn Ford, Kelly Galloup, Rusty Gates, Bill Halliday, Dawn Kemp, Art Neumann, Carol Neuman, Kelly Neuman, Steve Nevala, the Anglers of the Au Sable, Huron National Forest District Ranger Office in Mio, Michigan, Department of Natural Resources—especially Dave Smith and Steve Sendek, the Institute for Fisheries Research in Ann Arbor, and to all my friends who balance the books with volunteered effort, those who wade cold and deep and never whine.

Special thanks to the following fly tiers for their contributions for the fly plates: Sam Surre, Jerry Regan, Rock Wilson, Kelly Galloup, Kelly Neuman, Jac Ford, Vaughn Snook, Rusty Gates, Gates Au Sable Lodge, The Fly Factory.

In Memoriam: Bill Halliday and George Griffith

◆

**Series Editor:** Frank Amato—Kim Koch

Subscriptions:
Softbound: $35.00 for one year (four issues) $65.00 for two years
Hardbound Limited Editions: $95.00 one year, $170.00 for two years

Photography: Robert Linsenman (unless otherwise noted)
Fly plates photographed by: Jim Schollmeyer
Design: Kathy Johnson
Map: Kathy Johnson
Softbound ISBN: 1-57188-093-3, Hardbound ISBN: 1-57188-094-1

Kolka Creek

Bradford Creek

Frederic

To Upper Peninsula

I–75

Au Sable River

M–72

Grayling

M–72

I–75

To Detroit

No. Down River Road

Mainstream

"Holy

Water"

Stephan Bridge

Wakely Bridge Road

River Road

Chase Bridge Road

So. Down

Roscommon

South Branch Au Sable River

Mason Tract

Lovells

North Branch Au Sable River

West Branch Big Creek

Middle Branch Big Creek

East Branch Big Creek

No. Down River Road

F–32 / 608

489

Parmalee Bridge

Mio Pond

McKin

Cherry Creek    Road

Au    Sable    River

Au    Sable    River

Big Creek

M–55

M–72

Mio

M–55

So.

Luzerne

M–72

F–97

McMaster's Bridge Road

M–18/F–97

1 2 3 4 5 6 7 8 9 10 11 12 13 14 15 16 17 18 19 20 21 22 23 24 25 26

*Above: Tiny brook trout—an overachiever.*
*Middle: Big fish running.*
*Right: The author caught this 30-inch buck on a small Hex nymph.*

RICK KUSTICH

*Fall colors are stunning throughout the river's course.*

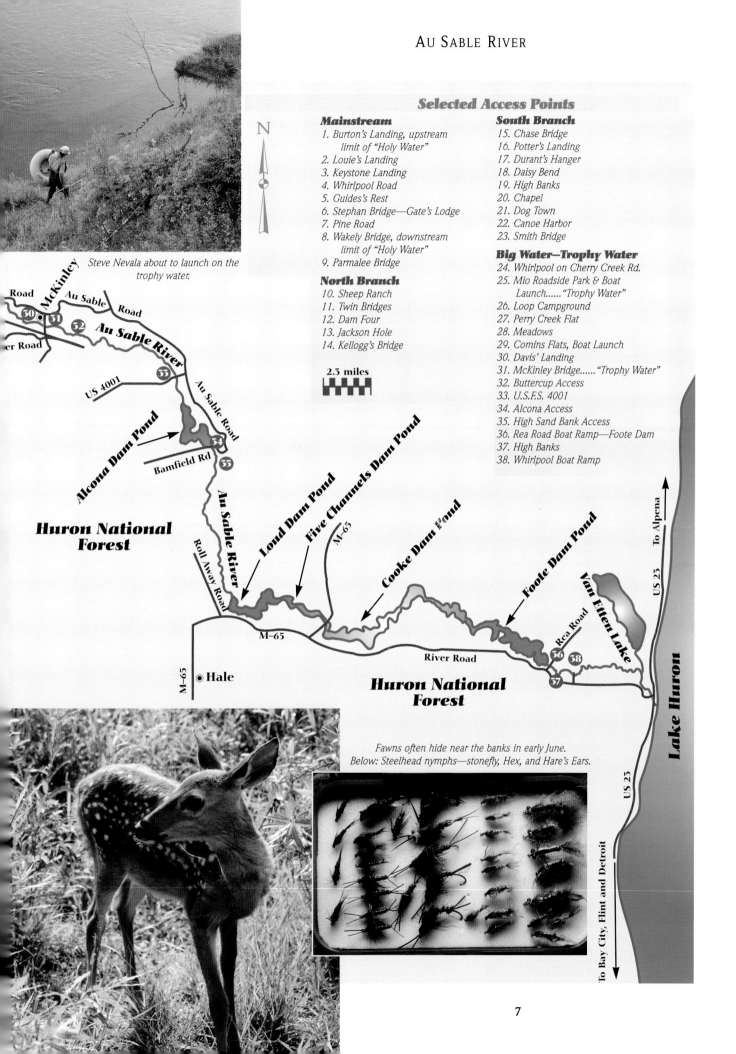

Steve Nevala about to launch on the trophy water.

## Selected Access Points

### Mainstream
1. Burton's Landing, upstream limit of "Holy Water"
2. Louie's Landing
3. Keystone Landing
4. Whirlpool Road
5. Guides's Rest
6. Stephan Bridge—Gate's Lodge
7. Pine Road
8. Wakely Bridge, downstream limit of "Holy Water"
9. Parmalee Bridge

### North Branch
10. Sheep Ranch
11. Twin Bridges
12. Dam Four
13. Jackson Hole
14. Kellogg's Bridge

2.3 miles

### South Branch
15. Chase Bridge
16. Potter's Landing
17. Durant's Hanger
18. Daisy Bend
19. High Banks
20. Chapel
21. Dog Town
22. Canoe Harbor
23. Smith Bridge

### Big Water—Trophy Water
24. Whirlpool on Cherry Creek Rd.
25. Mio Roadside Park & Boat Launch......"Trophy Water"
26. Loop Campground
27. Perry Creek Flat
28. Meadows
29. Comins Flats, Boat Launch
30. Davis' Landing
31. McKinley Bridge......"Trophy Water"
32. Buttercup Access
33. U.S.F.S. 4001
34. Alcona Access
35. High Sand Bank Access
36. Rea Road Boat Ramp—Foote Dam
37. High Banks
38. Whirlpool Boat Ramp

Fawns often hide near the banks in early June.
Below: Steelhead nymphs—stonefly, Hex, and Hare's Ears.

7

*Cobaka looks for risers.*

# Au Sable River

My father employed a simple but effective classification for the trout waters in proximity to our lake cabin in Oscoda County. There were many creeks—Houghton, Wilkins, Klacking—but only one river—the Au Sable. If he announced a trip to "the creeks," I was joyous because he would most often take me along and I could dangle red worms on tiny hooks into the dark swirls near cedar stumps. Sometimes there would be a tap-tap-tap and I would yell and yank and launch a small trout into the willows. My father would praise me and I began to appreciate the fact that being a kid in Michigan was a sweet deal. But on many afternoons, in late June especially, the kid karma turned sour. My father would fuss over his dry flies, stretch leaders, dress a fly line and stare at the sky. This meant "the river," and I would be staying home. "You're too young yet, too small for the Au Sable." In my small, curtained-off bedroom I would shake and curse silently. I hated the Au Sable River and I really hated being six, seven, eight and nine years old.

July 26, 1953 is as clear in my mind as Neil Armstrong's first step on the moon. It was my tenth birthday and my father gave me an eight-foot fly rod, a Medalist reel, an HDH line, and a plastic box with a dozen flies. "Would you like to go to 'the river' with me this afternoon?"

My mother said quietly, with no room for debate, "Carl, you are going to ruin that kid." That day I caught a rainbow trout on a dry fly at Perry Creek Flat below Mio and was ruined for life.

More than 40 years have passed and, true to form, I sit near a streamside spread of wild iris at the edge of a deep, silt-bottomed pool. It is late June, still hot, muggy, and nearly full daylight at 9 p.m. I have been waiting anxiously for nearly an hour, but the bugs will not be hurried. Patience is the key to the retention of any shred of sanity during the Hex hatch.

Variously called Michigan caddis, Michigan mayfly,

Canadian soldier, or simply Hex, the *Hexagenia limbata* at 2 1/2 inches in length is the grand kahuna of North American mayflies. After two years in their silt burrows the nymphs rise to the surface—slowly, undulating, taunting, riding the current drying and fluttering in the late evening. If a Hendrickson reminds you of a sailboat, the Hex dun will look like a 30-meter yacht. But it is the spinner fall that excites the largest trout in the river, browns and rainbows that normally eat large sculpins, crayfish, and other trout. The spinners come in waves, in the tens of thousands, and the trout line up and feed like hogs. Some rises out there in the gloom sound like the flush of an industrial strength toilet, some like a fat spaniel jumping off a dock, some like a soft, wet kiss. Last year, an unflappable Welshman known widely for droll understatement turned to me as the fish began to feed and fairly shrieked, "This is goddamned bloody exciting!" Indeed.

Downstream about 30 yards, my good friend Steve Nevala is fishing, organizing two cans of beer, his float tube, a cigar, floatant, a clip-on flashlight, and a collection of his new "totally secret" spinner pattern. He is muttering. I check my leader, my fly, test the flashlight, and note the time—10:15. A fish rises in midstream. Another. What's that sound? "Jesus!" Steve calls. "Here they come!" A pulsing hum like a low RPM electric motor fills the air—the sound of thousands upon thousands of Hex spinners. Overhead are falling, flexing clouds of lust. We are at the *limbata* dance in downtown Hexaritaville. It's show time.

## Timber Gold and Grayling

One hundred and fifty years ago, the Au Sable valley was enveloped in the shade of Michigan's magnificent white pines. They reached over 100 feet in height and achieved diameters

*Kelly Galloup demonstrates nymphing techniques on the Big Water.*

Guide party on the Au Sable at Dewey's Landing, 1887. Chief David Shoppengon, at right on the ground, a Chippewa who came to the Grayling area in the mid-1870s and guided lumber buyers and other visitors. Picture center, in white shirt, president of Chicago Board of Trade. Photo courtesy of The Fly Factory.

◆

well beyond six feet. The forest sea appeared an endless roll with gentle slopes conveniently cut by a navigable river. The river had been variously named *Riviere aux Sable*, Sandy, Sand, and *Beauvais* River by white explorers, but by the early 1800s the French name, Au Sable (meaning river of sand) had

◆

The aftermath of clear-cutting the forest . surrounding the North Branch of the Au Sable. Photo courtesy of Art Neumann.

achieved status with map makers. The Ottawa and Chippewa name, Mud-au-bee-be-ton-ange, "Flowing from the interior to the lake," described the perfect highway for floating logs to the mills on Lake Huron. The valley was a lumberman's perfect dream at one dollar per acre.

Between 1860 and 1900, the lumber industry boomed in the Au Sable valley. During that period, Michigan produced over 200 billion board feet of timber—enough to cover the entire state with pine boards one inch thick, build 50 roads 16 feet wide and one-inch thick from New York to San Francisco, and have several millions of board feet left over. Michigan's timber rebuilt Chicago after the fire, and the dollar value of this "timber gold" was one billion more than all the gold mined in California.

The river was changed forever by the scouring and scraping of the massive logs, by sand erosion from naked hillsides, by tons of sediment and the build-up of silt flats, and by the awakening interest of the sporting public.

Early railroad and rough "jack pine trails" cut through the wilderness to the valley, and anglers came to catch and kill grayling. Like the buffalo and passenger pigeon, the Au Sable's native grayling seemed without limit. They were beautiful, more importantly gullible, and most importantly, finite. Michigan grayling, *Thymallus tricolor*, brought tourist dollars from Chicago, New York, Philadelphia, Detroit, England, and beyond. Recognizing the market value in a name, the citizens of the small village of Crawford on the river's banks changed the town name to Grayling and the sporting boom accelerated.

Anglers used three and four flies on their leaders and most casts produced a fish on each fly. The sportsmen caught them by the hundreds, day after day after day. Tons were sold to restaurants at 25 cents per pound. More tons were left to rot on the banks in a mockery of sporting ethics. Even Rube Babbit, Michigan's first game warden and a guide on the river, sold fish. The last Au Sable grayling was caught in 1908.

Rainbow trout were first planted in 1876 by Dan Fitzhugh of Bay City; the first recorded brook trout planting was in 1885, by Rube Babbit, and brown trout made it to the Au Sable in the late 1880s. Early regulations dictated a six-inch size limit and a daily bag of 50. The brook trout had difficulty keeping up, but the more secretive and selective brown trout flourished.

Early conservationists fought their battles straight uphill. William Mershon of Saginaw was an articulate, thoughtful, and tireless voice for conservation in the very early 1900s. Daniel Fitzhugh of Bay City began his fight to save the grayling as early as 1871 and continued to counsel on behalf of the river and trout to the end of his days.

More recently George Mason, George Griffith, Art Neumann, and a small cadre of radical thinkers have made a

*Lovells and the North Branch of Au Sable, circa 1908 photo, after clear cutting the surrounding forest. Photo courtesy of Art Neumann.*

significant and positive impact—George Mason with a magnificent gift of land and inspiration, George Griffith and Art Neumann as the pioneer founders of Trout Unlimited and most recently, The Anglers of the Au Sable, with the revolutionary notions of flies-only, no-kill and simple mathematics—if you release fish unharmed, there will be more left than if you kill them.

Michigan's early history is centered on rivers, the opportunities, responsibilities, and passions inspired by water atilt. The early guides and fly tiers, Rube Babbit, David Shoppenagon, Charlie Shellenbarger, Henry Stephan, Len Jewell, Clarence Roberts, Jack Schwiegert and the revolutionary conservationists, Mershon, Fitzhugh and Mason among others, pattern the intricate weave of history with colorful paths along the Au Sable's banks. Like the grayling, they are now gone to echoes and ghosts in the trees.

## The River System

Thanks to the ice age and the incalculable grinding power of glaciers, Michigan has the largest coastline of any state excluding Alaska, more than 11,000 lakes, and over 36,000 miles of streams and rivers. More than 20 percent of the world's fresh water supply flows through Michigan and there is no geographic point in the state that is more than six miles from a stream, river, or lake. And it snows and snows and rains—and then rains some more. We Michiganders are a soggy bunch.

There is water everywhere, falling

*The Au Sable circa 1950. Photo courtesy of Art Neumann.*

*A classic Au Sable River boat on the Holy Water.*

◆

on our heads and squishing under our feet, draining into a rivulet, then a creek, on to a river, and eventually feeding one of the Great Lakes. A lot of this moving water is justifiably famous. Chief Pontiac, America's highest-ranking cannibal, terrorized the British from the Detroit River. The Pere Marquette is one of the nation's premier steelhead streams, the Muskegon is an incredible tailwater trout fishery, the Manistee is a year-round treasure with steelhead, salmon, and superb brown trout angling. And there are many more—the

Pigeon, the Sturgeon, the Escanaba, the Two-Hearted, The Fox, The St. Mary's. But for a high percentage of the fly angling public, resident as well as tourist, the term "the river" refers to only one, the majestic Au Sable. My river.

The river's official birthplace is the junction of Bradford and Kolka creeks near the village of Frederick due north of Grayling. From this point, the flow meanders south to Grayling, makes a sharp, eastward turn, picks up the flow of the East Branch and continues its easterly run to Lake Huron.

◆

*George Mason circa 1950. Photo courtesy of Art Neumann.*

Throughout its course, the Au Sable system comes together and swells that small stream born near Frederick. It is fed by numerous brooks and several significant tributaries, and is continually charged by the countless ground springs bubbling up from the Marshall and Coldwater-Antrim aquifers. In fact, the Au Sable is a spring creek, one of the five largest ground-spring rivers in North America.

Just east of the Grayling city limits, Burton's Landing marks the upstream boundary of the flies-only, no-kill water, the eight-mile flow to Wakeley Bridge, known as "the Holy Water." Approximately three river-miles downstream from Wakeley Bridge, the South Branch of the Au Sable merges a fertile and significant volume of water. From this point it is four-plus river-miles to McMaster's Bridge, then another two miles to the confluence with the North Branch. With the addition of the flows from the South Branch and the North Branch, the hydrodynamics of the river are swollen dramatically, evidential of the powerful surge farther downstream. What was a happy and friendly spring creek just a few miles upstream has become a vigorous, powerful river that is unforgiving to carefree or foolish behavior.

This is the official starting point for "the Big Water." It is approximately seven miles from the North Branch to the access point at Parmalee Bridge, then another three miles to the mouth of the northward run of Big Creek at Big Creek Flat. From there the last of the river's free flow is the four miles to the backwater pond behind the dam at Mio, the first in a series of Consumer's Energy generating plants on the course to Lake Huron. Below Mio the river widens but does not slow its pace on the way to the next obstacle, roughly 35 miles downstream, Alcona Dam. In this stretch the tributaries are smallish brook trout headwaters. Loud Creek, Perry Creek, O'Brien Creek, and others make contributions, but the noticeable increase in volume is more attributable to the influx of water from ground springs in the riverbed and along the banks.

This stretch of river is big trout habitat with deep, foreboding holes, long, inky flats, and lively, oxygenated riffles over a streambed of sand, fine and course gravel, rock, and silt. But during mid- to late summer, afternoon water temperatures reach well into the 70s, and although the springs, riffles, and deep holes provide cooling safety, the backwaters of Alcona Pond are the downstream limit for the Au Sable's classic trout water.

From Alcona the river flows nearly due south approximately 12 miles to the backwaters of Loud Dam. This flow is a mixed fishery with walleye, trout, and superb fly angling for smallmouth bass. Hoppy Creek, the South Branch River (not to be confused with the South Branch of the Au Sable), Smith Creek, and Stewart Creek enter the Au Sable on this flow to the next impoundment.

Between Loud Dam and Foote Dam, the Au Sable is not so much a river; it is more a continuing backwater of varying width. The outflow from Loud Dam Pond feeds almost immediately into the pond known as Five Channels Dam Pond, then into Cooke Dam Pond, and finally into Foote Dam Pond. Foote

*Dan Tooman poles through a turn near Burton's Landing.*

◆

Dam is the last of the hydroelectric facilities on the river.

From Foote to Lake Huron, the Au Sable has several miles of unimpeded flow. This last reach of river is famous for large, kinetic steelhead and heavy runs of salmon. Although it is generally too warm to sustain a year-round trout population, it provides excellent angling for walleye and smallmouth bass with northern pike and whitefish as a bonus.

In this overview of the river we have followed the course well over 100 miles. At its headwaters the Au Sable is a child's splashy skip from bank to bank. In the Holy Water it is a beautiful, critical paramour. The South Branch is both brook trout nursery and haven to hook-jawed browns as long as your arm. The clean, cool run of the North Branch is a beckoning, comfortable stream with prolific hatches and guileless brookies. The Big Water demands your attention to detail and a good measure of common sense regarding safety, but its gifts are extravagant. The steelhead reach below Foote Dam is the birthplace of the Great Lakes strain. These direct descendants of the McCloud River, first stocked over 100 years ago, are the most beautiful and powerful steelhead in the Great Lakes basin. But more about all of this, lots more, a bit later.

*Tight looping on the Holy Water.*

◆

## The Mainstream
## "The Holy Water"

Steve Nevela and I stood at the foot of the stairs at the Whirlpool in the upper Holy Water. A very few brown drake duns struggled into the air and already we could see a few splashy rises and the sub-surface glint of larger fish turning on nymphs.

As usual you often hear the approach of a canoe before you see it. In this case it was not the hollow clang of aluminum on wood or rock, it was shrill and frustrated harangue. The East Coast accent and the slurred speech were both evident long before the woman slammed the nose of the canoe into the logs near our feet. She was wet and high octane mad. The fat teenager in the bow grinned madly and popped a fresh can of beer. "Is this Louie's Landing," she shrieked, "Are you the @!&* guys from Hutt's that take out the canoes?"

"This isn't Louie's Landing," I answered.

"Do you guys take out canoes?" she asked.

"We've often considered it, but no," Steve said.

"Where is Louie's Landing, goddamn it!"

"Upstream. You've passed it."

I guess this turned out well enough. We advised the "lady" that she could either get out here and hike, or proceed down to Stephan Bridge and politely ask to use the phone at Gate's Au Sable Lodge to call for a pick-up. As she paddled into the dusk she screamed at the kid, then, turned and suggested that "All you *&#! Michigan hicks should go &@!%." Her voice faded into the river. "Rusty's going to *love* her," Steve said. "Let's fish."

The Holy Water, that reach of the mainstream from just east of Grayling at Burton's Landing downstream eight miles to Wakely Bridge, received the blessing of "no-kill, flies-only" regulations in 1988. The hard-fought victory came only after an intensive, exhausting effort by enlightened conservationists led by the Anglers of the Au Sable. The campaign involved business interests, anglers, politicians, and journalists at every level—from local to national. It featured acrimony, passion, physical threats (including the poisoning of the river by anonymous and dimwitted opponents), massive letter writing operations, and political and scientific turmoil.

Today, all trout must be immediately released, unharmed. All fishing must be with artificial flies and, although the Department of Natural Resources does not so require, it is recommended that all hooks be barbless.

The Holy Water is the heart of the river, the pump that pushes cold, crystalline renewal downstream. Its fragile beauty is stunning. It is easy to wade and fish, and is easily accessed at multiple public sites. It draws anglers from around the world.

At Burton's Landing the river is about 45 feet wide with silt edges and a firm bottom of sand and mixed gravel. The holding water is, for the most part, easy to identify, but it is worthwhile to fish all the water very thoroughly. Often the browns, and particularly the brook trout, will move into the clear, shallow flow at the edges of more traditionally promising water. Be sure to cast your fly to the shadowed banks, to the small pockets at the base of stumps, and under the protective sweepers. If there is no hatch, fish a small sculpin pattern with a hard, snappy retrieve, a caddis emerger with an across and down swing, or a small pheasant tail on a pure, dead-drift. The water is very clear and the trout are not reckless.

The stretch from Louie's Landing past Keystone Landing, the Whirlpool, Thendara Road, and Guide's Rest to Stephan Bridge is arguably the most lovely and diverse reach of the Holy Water. Some of the tight curves build and hold water to necktie depth while most runs level out at mid-thigh. The bottom is firm sand and fine to medium gravel—perfect habitat for caddis, olives, Hendricksons, sulphurs, brown drakes, and a variety of stoneflies. The flow flexes and spreads from 40 to 65 feet in width and is bordered, in large part, by private vacation cottages and year-round homes.

At Guide's Rest, accessible from North Down River Road between Whirlpool Road and Stephan Bridge Road, there is a long stretch that, if not totally wild, is certainly less civilized and tamed. Here the angler's sensation is of being in a time warp, perhaps transported back to a simpler age. There are fewer noticeable intrusions of the very late 20th century, there are more tangled sweepers, and the bank is moss, cedar, and wild flowers rather than manicured grass.

There is a growing controversy, with no small amount of spirited discussion, that concerns the number of large trout in the Holy Water. The number *seems* to be decreasing and this is a source of great frustration to the angling faithful. Accusing fingers point in many directions: at the rental canoe overload, at the Camp Grayling military installation, at the canoe marathon, at the slow degradation of in-stream, woody structures, and

*Steve Southard, owner of The Fly Factory and Ray's Conoe Livery.*

*Rusty Gates, dedicated river guardian, at his shop.*

ridiculously, at the "no-kill" regulations.

It is my opinion, shared with many, that the answer is relatively simple. This section of the river is overused; it is stressed and so are the trout. The large fish, mostly browns, either move downstream to bigger water where they can more effectively evade commotion, or adapt their feeding patterns to accommodate prevailing conditions. This means they behave "naturally" only when conditions suit them, when they are not stressed—on cloudy, cool days, during a rain, early morning, late evenings, and at night. These are periods and conditions that entice smaller numbers of human intruders. The trout have adapted, but we anglers have been slow to make the adjustment. We would all prefer to cast dry flies on a pretty, warm day, exactly the kind of day that attracts the aluminum bullets. Too much clanging, too many frightening shadows cause the fish to hide and sulk. This may be a gross oversimplification, but it is my opinion and I'm sticking to it.

On a pleasant day in July of 1996 I floated the Holy Water with guide Dan Tooman. The expressed purpose was to take photographs for this book, but as it turned out we had the opportunity to test the "overload theory" as well. For whatever reason, known only to the Higher Power, there were very few canoes on the river. There was no hatch—no midges in the air, no fluttering caddis, no stoneflies, no olives. It was too early for Tricos.

Dan and I huddled briefly and decided to try big streamers. A size 4 olive Zoo Cougar was selected and Dan pushed the graceful Au Sable boat into the current. We fished the pockets near wood structure, the deep holes, the dark gurgles beneath the sweepers, and the undercut banks. We cast with force—slapping the fly on the water and stripping with fast, erratic jerks.

The trout showed. Not all of them ate the fly, but over 20 good fish swirled, bumped, chased, or otherwise let us know that they were indeed interested in a mouthful. Several fish were in the mid-teens and one fish that slid out from an undercut bank was close enough to 20 inches. When we reached the take-out below Wakely Bridge we were both pretty pleased. I had some workable photographs, and we had moved an impressive number of large trout. On the float from Burton's Landing to Wakely Bridge we had seen only three other anglers, two canoes, and one work crew installing a large log and stump fish cover. We drank a glass of lemonade in the warm afternoon sunshine. "Can I have one of your Zoo Cougars?" Dan asked.

Gate's Au Sable Lodge sits on the south bank of the river at Stephan Bridge. This is Mecca to the angling faithful—the epicenter of Holy Water devotionals—with comfortable streamside lodging, a restaurant, and a complete fly shop. Rusty and Julie Gates own the joint and dispense thoughtful, accurate information on current and anticipated conditions. Rusty is the president of The Anglers of the Au Sable and was named Angler of the Year in 1995 by *Fly Rod & Reel* magazine for his efforts on behalf of the river as a living ecosystem.

From Stephan Bridge to Wakely Bridge the river builds size and presents a stronger, more serious character. It retains great beauty and an inviting demeanor, but the riffles are quicker, the runs deeper, and the dark holes are more numerous.

The superb book, *The Bird in the Waterfall* by Jerry Dennis, presents various distinctions between streams and rivers and refers to the 1896 short story "Crocker's Hole" by R.D. Blackmore. The author asks, " 'But what is the test of a river?' 'The power to drown a man,' replies the river darkly." Between Stephan and Wakely bridges the Au Sable grows from a stream into a river.

Hatches are prolific in this reach and it is here where most of the larger trout showed during the Zoo Cougar float mentioned earlier. The early season (mid-April to mid-May) presents reliable hatches of olives, black caddis, mahogany drakes, and Hendricksons. Additionally, because the water is still very cool and daytime air temperatures are not high enough to attract large numbers of recreational canoers, mid-day angling with large streamers, Woolly Buggers, and soft-hackle wets is often rewarding. But this is the time of year when the urge to fish dry-fly patterns begins to peak and the insects and trout should be ready to indulge. A black or smoky gray Delta-winged Caddis with a bright green egg sack on a size 18 hook often brings eager fish to the surface from (about) late April through mid-May. Size 18 and 20 Parachute Olives effectively mimic the *Baetis vagans* during the same period.

◆

*Habitat work near Wakely Bridge.*

Mahogany duns (*Paraleptophlebia adoptiva*) in size 16 produce good numbers of fish during the first two weeks of May, and, dependent on weather, the Hendricksons bring even larger trout to hand.

Late May through June is magic time on the Holy Water. Hendricksons are still on the water when the first *dorothea* sulphurs make their appearance. These pale yellow (size 16 and 18) bugs are consistent in their evening curtain calls and reliably attractive to surprisingly large fish. The "drakes," meaning brown drake *simulans',* have a relatively short run of about 10 days, but they are a long-anticipated sensation. "Brown drake fever" is serious and as reliable as a Christmas cold or the flu. Everybody gets it—at the same time. Now we are talking about big flies (size 10) and big fish, the biggest, coming together in the cooling air and failing light of late evening. The guides are booked and the clients are twitchy. Long leaders are shortened, fine tippets are replaced with 2X and the trophy log book on the counter in Gates' fly shop begins to fill.

Although a few Hex straggle through the reach, the Holy Water, for the most part, is not prime *limbata* habitat. The mid- to late-summer fly fishing centers more on Cahills, various olives, green oak worms and assorted other terrestrials, caddis, stoneflies, and Tricos. And streamers remain effective under low-light or low-traffic conditions.

The Holy Water is dream water, an outrageous beauty that grows through exuberant, innocent youth at Burton's Landing to a mature, sultry, sometimes sullen temptress at Wakely Bridge. It has mothered inspiration as the birthplace of Trout Unlimited (you might doff your cap or salute as you pass by the Barbless Hook, George Griffith's home just upstream from Wakely), and centers today's controversy and debate over the concept of fair use of the resource. A river is a living thing of incalculable value in and of itself. In my experience there is no place on earth where this fact is more clearly evident than the Holy Water.

*Jac Ford comtemplating a change.*

## Wakely to McMasters

As the river passes beneath Wakely Bridge and pushes toward its confluence with the South Branch of the Au Sable, the angler will sense a slight decrease in the hydraulic gradient, and will notice a slow but steady increase of black silt along the edges. There is a mix of water types through this stretch. Deep holes with stumps, logs, and shade from sweepers, fast runs with gravel bottoms, and smooth pools of moderate depth provide cover for brown, brook, and a few rainbow trout.

The increasing amount of noticeable silt is important. Although olives, mahoganys, brown drakes, caddis, and stoneflies are still abundant and important players, the *Hexagenia limbata* moves to center stage.

Dependent on weather (warm is good), *limbata* nymphs with fluttering philoplume tails and gills will begin to attract larger fish around the first of June. Being efficient predators, trout prefer to key on specific, dominant prey items, so they will selectively eat the hatch *du jour*; as an example, it is my

experience that the large *limbata* patterns will not work during brown drake activity but, other than that obvious exception, the *limbata* nymphs on size 6 and 8 hooks are an effective searching pattern for substantial trout.

Roughly halfway between Wakely and McMasters bridges, the South Branch converges with the main stream. The resultant increase in volume is significant. Nearly doubled in size, the Au Sable pushes outward and down with a wider, deeper flow and a formidable disposition. And as the river pushes downstream to Connor's Flat, the amount of silt expands considerably.

This black muck that shelters the burrowing *Hexagenia* seems to fan the flames of mania in both local and visiting fly fishers. Big fish cover and big bug habitat add up to an astounding angler dementia in late June. The automobile license plates at the accesses and in the fly shop parking lots represent a dozen or more states and the anglers seem to be in a semi-hypnotic state.

The "Hex Vex" first infected me 40 years ago. My father's vacation had not yet started and my mother, sister, and I were at our cabin on Island Lake while he worried the automobile production at Fisher Body.

During a grocery run to Mio, I wandered into a small log

Hexagenia limbata *bring the river's largest trout to the surface.*

◆

shop. The sign above the door read, "Boyd Sentner Flies—Rocks." The man behind the counter seemed to be in his mid-fifties. He started off with a bit of growl in his voice that day, but as I asked my endless questions he responded with more and more warmth. He showed me parachute olives on tiny hooks, meaty Brown Drake duns, parachute Cahills, and his pride and joy, the clipped deer-hair Hex spinners on size 2 and 4 hooks. He had extended-body Hex patterns with long horse-mane tails, eggsacks, and fan wings of white calf tail, and cream-bodied parachutes with white posts.

If my memory is accurate, the big flies cost 50 cents each and I had only enough change in my pocket for two. But I left his shop with a gift and an invitation. The flat plastic box he gave me held four of the deer-hair monsters and he promised to take me (assuming my mother's permission) to fish the hatch at Connor's Flat the following evening.

He locked the door to his shop at precisely 8 p.m. and we were on the bank downstream from the access 40 minutes later. The river here is 70 to 85 feet wide with the deepest channel near the middle of the river, so I was instructed to stay close to the bank and to pick and pay strict attention to specific feeding fish. But first we waited, and waited some more.

Waiting through eternity is a tough assignment for a teenager. Two river boats took up positions near us on the downstream side and several anglers appeared, then spread out along the banks. I remember muffled talk, pipe smoke, the smell of "6-12" bug dope, and the crawl of time as darkness fell. I wanted to wade out and make a few practice casts but Mr. Sentner cautioned patience. "Don't move out yet. You might spook a fish that wants to feed in close," he said. I checked my tippet knot for the hundredth time and waited some more.

When darkness finally enveloped us it offered no moon glow, no starlight to even faintly define distance. The only suggestion of perspective and dimension came from the soft sound of the river or an infrequent, muffled voice. Then the air was filled with spinners more than two inches long. They were in my hair, crawling on my neck and hands. Then they were on the water and the fish began to feed. Time condenses from this point. The span from 10:30 p.m., when the trout began to feed, to about 12:30 a.m., when they quit rising, took all of five minutes.

Fish were hooked, lost and landed all around me. Mr. Sentner released two and kept one of about 17 inches. A man in one of the boats cursed softly after a heavy splash. Three trout fed wildly just a few feet from me, but I never figured out their cycle, and worse, I abandoned my orders to pick out one and stay with it. Too excited. "Calm down. You're casting too much. Listen." It was Sentner's voice, but it was too late. It was a fishless night for me, but still one of high reward with the promise of many more to come.

The large mayflies take star billing in this section of the Au Sable, but there are other prey items that provide substantial amounts of protein for the trout. Shiners, dace, chubs, blunt-nose and fathead minnows, sticklebacks, sculpins, darters, and crayfish are important forage. Streamers tied to copy shiners, dace, and sculpins seduce more than a few large browns over the course of the season. Weighted crayfish patterns are tied on less frequently, but if hopped and crawled along the bottom in the dark of night, are very effective. From Wakely to McMasters, the river moves from a series of pools and riffles to a smooth, consistent run. It swells with the inflow of the South Branch and moves from a predominantly sand, gravel, cobble bottom to one of sand and silt with some clay. Through this course the river's gradient is moderate (ranging from three to nine feet/mile), the habitat sustains some very large trout, and if your timing is right, the fishing will combine suspense and excitement without parallel.

## The South Branch

The headwaters of the South Branch begin at the outflow of Lake St. Helen in southeastern Roscommon County at an elevation of 1,156 feet. From there the river follows a northerly meander for 37 miles to its junction with the mainstream at 1,035 feet of elevation. The drop of just over 100 feet in nearly 40 miles produces a smooth, even flow interspersed with lively riffles. The wading is generally comfortable and the fishing, particularly in the Mason Tract, is good throughout the season and superb during the major hatches.

The Mason Tract consists of 2,860 acres, 1,500 of which were bequeathed to the State of Michigan by the estate of George Mason in 1955. Mason died in 1954 and his gift provides public ownership of 11-plus river miles of beautiful and productive trout water. Much of the surrounding lands are federal forest. Homes, cabins and other man-made structures have either been removed or allowed to disintegrate, and the natural forest has been permitted to rejuvenate and heal the land.

In addition to the land gift, Mason funded the construction of The Fisherman's Chapel on the river's east bank as a place for quiet reflection. Construction was completed in 1960 and since that time, the chapel has welcomed wedding parties, baptisms, eulogies, and countless, peaceful meditations of anglers from around the world. In addition to this magnificent gift, Mason was the inspirator of Trout Unlimited. When you visit the South Branch take a moment to whisper a "thank you."

At Lake St. Helen the river curves north and west to the village of Roscommon, then north to Steckart Bridge where it turns northeast into the beginning of the Mason Tract at Chase Bridge. From Roscommon to Steckart Bridge the bottom is mostly sand and there is heavy habitat impact from residential development. The sand continues past Steckart, but gravel and riffle combinations increase as the river nears Chase Bridge and the upstream boundary of the Mason Tract.

From Chase Bridge to Canoe Harbor (just a short distance from Hwy M-72 and Smith Bridge) the protecting shield of Mason's gift provides a rewarding, near pristine experience for the fly angler. The surrounding hillsides, valleys, and swales are alive with birds and game, wildflowers, and a stunning array of trees.

River access points are numerous and easy to find throughout the tract. Beginning at Chase Bridge some of the more popular points are Durant's Castle, Daisy Bend, High Banks, Mason Chapel, Baldwin's, Downey's, Dog Town, and Canoe Harbor near the tract's downstream boundary. The volume of flow builds through this reach but remains accommodating to the wading angler. Near Chase Bridge the river averages 50 feet in width and varies from that measure, contracting and expanding its channel throughout its course.

Aquatic insects are abundant and their hatches are reliable and relatively constant throughout the season. Olives, little black caddis, Hendricksons, sulphurs, brown drakes, Hex, *Isonychia*, and Tricos produce top-quality angling during their respective emergence periods. Several species of stoneflies, terrestrials, mice, and forage fish add substantial protein to the mix. Mottled and slimy sculpin, chubs, dace, darters, and shiners along with crayfish and immature trout form the base menu for some of the largest brown trout in the entire Au Sable system.

Beginning in mid-May the South Branch stabilizes in volume (there is a control dam at the outlet of Lake St. Helens and the early season flows can fluctuate widely), temperatures moderate, and the hatches shift into overdrive. Hendricksons and little black caddis are the earliest to consistently produce surface feeding activity. And the Hendricksons have enough size to merit attention from larger trout.

A typical day in mid-May will provide emerging black caddis sometime before noon with mating and egg laying from about noon through the early afternoon. The females carry a bright green egg sack and seem to be favored by the brookies that dart up from the riffles and the browns that wait near the logs and sweepers. The insect's name is a bit misleading. Although it appears black in the air and on the water, the actual color is dark smoke. The most productive patterns will be tied on 16 and 18 hooks with a dusky slate body, sooty, iron-gray wings, and the bright green egg-ball.

Depending on temperature, this same day will show Hendrickson emergers and duns from noon on toward late afternoon. Typically, the spinner falls occur in late afternoon and early evening, but during exceptionally warm periods, may take place at dawn. Both *Ephemerella subvaria* and *rotunda* species are present in the South Branch, and to complicate matters just a bit more, the mahogany dun (*Paraleptophlabia adoptiva*), smaller and very similar in coloration, may overlap with both emerging duns and spinner falls.

*A five-inch baby rainbow pattern fooled this trophy hen.*

*Above: Doc calls in for his messages: "Tell him to take two aspirin and call me after the* Hex *hatch."*
*Right: A size 1 chartreuse Woolly Sculpin is often effective.*

*Wild iris mean the* Hex *hatch is near.*

*Midday trophies come to streamers and* simulans *and* limbata *nymphs.*

◆

Two local patterns, Rusty's Spinner and Borcher's Special, will effectively cover the dun and spinner requirements for Hendricksons as well as mahoganys, and also produce well during brown drake and *Isonychia* activity. A selection of each of the flies in sizes 16 through 10 is good insurance on the South Branch. Not infrequently, the larger brown trout will become critical and very selective during the Hendrickson dun phase. When this occurs I have found that a no-hackle fly, such as those popularized by Doug Swisher and Carl Richards, will be accepted.

The sulphurs, both *invaria* and *dorothea*, make their initial appearance in late May and continue into June, often overlapping with the brown drakes. These pale yellow bugs, size 16 and 18 respectively, mark the transition of peak dry-fly fishing from afternoon to evening. The duns emerge quickly from gravel runs and riffles in the late afternoon and early evening. The variable in time of emergence is almost always keyed to temperature, but can be influenced by cloud cover as well. The spinner falls come right at dusk and provide the most enjoyable fishing (in my opinion). I have not found a high percentage of really large fish feeding on sulphurs (although a 16-inch trout is possible), so a light-line rod, say one of 9 feet for a three-weight line, is my choice for long leaders, fine tippets, and sulphur spinners on the South Branch.

The brown drakes start (usually) around the 5th of June and can run as late as the 20th. The winter and spring of 1996 was abnormally long and bitterly cold. The entire Au Sable system and, especially the South Branch, was off schedule and the hatches were late by as much as two weeks. Anglers that had hoped to fish the *Hexagenia limbata* spinner falls found themselves in the thick of brown drakes from Daisy Bend downstream to Dog Town, and from Smith Bridge to the main-stream, until the third week of June.

This is one of the "super hatches" of the South Branch. It places second only to the Hex madness and that fine point is debatable. *Ephemera simulans* is a burrower that requires a mix of sand and fine gravel under gentle runs and riffles. The duns typically emerge toward late evening, but can show sporadically throughout the day under heavy overcast. The spinners start right at dark and electrify the trout for about an hour. If the weather is exceptionally warm there may be only a brief, tentative mating swarm at the normal time, followed by a lull. Then, when the temperature cools, sometimes as late as midnight, a full-blown orgy results with a heavy spinner fall and aggressive gluttony.

Most anglers give up too early on hot evenings. "It's too hot. No hatch tonight," they say. They are almost always wrong. Wait it out. Believe me, a brown drake spinner fall under the soft glow of moonlight is worth it.

All the big fish and all the certifiable fly-fishing loonies come together for the Hex Vex on the South Branch. Beginning on, or around, June 18 and lasting through the first week of July, the Hex, a.k.a. Michigan caddis, giant Michigan mayfly, giant mayfly, Canadian soldier, giant yellow drake, and giant fish fly is center stage on the river, in the fly shops, restaurants and saloons, and in the hearts and minds of all fly anglers within praying distance of the Au Sable valley.

The flies are huge—the largest mayflies in North America. Immediately preceding emergence, the nymphs crowd two inches in length and require long shank hooks in sizes 4 and 6 for effective copies. They are burrowers and require silt and muck in order to thrive. In prime areas with dense populations, there may be as many as 1,000 nymph burrows within a square foot of the coal black ooze.

◆

*A sculpin pattern fooled this one.*

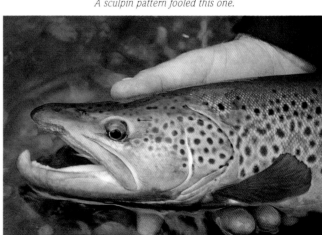

*Oops! The author has lost his grip.*

◆

Duns most often emerge from dusk to well past full darkness, but I remember many days of leaden overcast and drizzle with on-again/off-again emergences of struggling duns and slurping trout. Spinner falls also show some variation, but usually (almost always) take place in full darkness. It is important to note that Michigan is at the extreme western edge of the eastern time zone and in late June it is still twilight at 10:00 p.m.

The Hex spinner fall is a great shiver of excitement for the angler and is the hog trough of all banquets for large trout on the South Branch. Although long awaited, the first night's spinner fall is often a frustrating experience. The fish seem tentative and do not always respond with regular feeding patterns. The second night is a whole new chapter. Trout are expectant and aggressive and will sometimes rush several feet to take a quivering spinner during the early minutes of the fall. We anglers have shortened our leaders to six feet (or less) with a tippet of eight-pound test and are reasonably well prepared for the gluttonous surface feeding and our own attendant psychic transition to a mesmerized trance.

The near environs to Daisy Bend, High Banks, and Baldwin's are some of my favorites for the big bug dance. I look for long glides and runs close to heavy, overhung vegetation,

and, ideally, with logs and stumps nestled in the silt edges. Scout the water early and wait. Too much early nervous casting can disturb the trout. And you will have company. Other anglers will appear, and it is sound strategy to find your niche before darkness.

After two or three days the fish adjust to the big spinners and become more critical and selective. Pick a fish with a steady feeding rhythm, time the rises, and concentrate on that single fish. If the fish is trophy-sized, it will probably demand a drag-free float that puts the fly right between its eyes. Not to the right six inches, not to the left four inches—right between the eyes. If your fly drags, the fish will move on the first infraction, but keep feeding. Strike one. If the fly drags again, your trout will move again and probably resume feeding after a few minutes. Strike two. You get the idea.

Each year the South Branch produces extraordinary trophies and indelible memories during the brown drake, Hex and *Isonychia* hatches, but the Hex Vex is supreme on both counts. From Chase Bridge through the beautiful, wild Mason Tract and past Smith Bridge and the Oxbow Club on to the junction with the mainstream, the alluring pull of the giant mayflies is overpowering.

As good as the public access is throughout the Mason tract,

*The North Branch offers easy wading and wide-open casting.*

this ease of use does not continue on the remainder of the run to the mainstream. Beginning at Smith Bridge the riparian rights are largely with private landowners and entree to the water is problematic.

Here's a thought. Hire a guide for a full-day float for either the Mason tract or the lower run from Smith Bridge to the confluence. If the big flies are not on the menu you will probably enjoy olives, caddis, stoneflies, midges, and terrestrials on your eight-hour trip. You will have time to throw big sculpins, crayfish, and Woolly Buggers into the dark water under the sweepers and to the current seams at the edges of deep runs. You will fish beautiful water in good company, and you may touch and release a very large fish.

## The North Branch

The North Branch of the Au Sable is popular with anglers for its stable flow, cool water, diverse and prolific hatches, comfortable wading, and easy casting. Experts and novices alike find it a welcome respite from the often highly technical demands of the mainstream. It is a serene haven, relatively free of canoe traffic, and both the brook and brown trout are often eager to join our game.

It is an ideal classroom setting for instruction—beginners wade without fear, have ample room to practice their casting, and reliable hatches provide opportunities to "match" as well as understand and appreciate the insects' life cycle of nymph, emerger, dun and spinner.

The North Branch begins in Otsego County and flows southeasterly to the Crawford County line near Lewiston, then southerly to Lovells and on to its confluence with the Au Sable between McMasters and Parmalee. From its headwaters past Opal and Emerald lakes downstream to Dam Two north of Lovells, the North Branch is, for the most part, a flat, smooth run with a bottom dominated by sand. From Dam Two downstream throughout its remaining course, the river has more riffles, more shaded, bank-side holes, more gravel, more diverse and prolific hatches, and many more trout.

Flies-only regulations are in effect from the Sheep Ranch access just north of Lovells to the North Branch's junction with the mainstream approximately 21 miles downstream. An extended season allows angling until the end of October, and many anglers take advantage of his liberty to combine fly fishing and upland bird hunting in fall's blazing colors and crisp, sunny days.

Popular access points near Lovells include the Sheep Ranch, Twin Bridges (both just north of the village on F-97), and two DNR sites nearly in town. This is easy, pleasant water with gullible brook trout, good hatches, and consistent surface activity. Even during periods when aquatic insects are not in evidence, the fish will usually respond to a small Adams or soft hackle wet fly.

The Dam Four access, south and downstream from Lovells, has a good variety of cover types (both up and downstream from the parking area) with both brook and brown trout. The river is wide and affords easy wading and casting. It has a solid

bottom of gravel and sand and diverse species of mayflies and caddis.

The downstream reach is my favorite. The river has deep runs and riffles, well-shaded corner pockets and holes, and enough midstream stumps and depressions to provide cover for a substantial population of small to medium-sized fish. And there are some large, secretive browns in this reach—fish that surprise you with a long shadow during the day, or adjust your neck hair with a heavy rise in the black of night.

The campground at Jackson Hole is approximately seven miles south of Lovells (off F-97) and right on the river. Here the stream offers considerable variety in terms of width and depth. There are some tight corners and deep runs that provide excellent cover for larger fish, but they also make wading a bit dicey. This area has mahoganys, Hendricksons, little black caddis, some gray drakes, brown drakes, *Isonychia*, some *Hexagenia*, and a variety of stonefly species including the little yellow stonefly (yellow Sally) and the giant *dorsata*.

To many, the most intriguing fishing on the North Branch occurs during the trico explosion in late summer. These tiny flies are best imitated on size 22-26 hooks. The spinner pattern should have long, split tails of white artificial or stiff hackle fibers, white or clear wings, a white or cream abdomen, and a black thorax. Leaders need to be long and fine; usually a 7X tippet is about right. Use the "light" rod of your choice. My favorite is a 2-weight, medium-fast action, 8 1/2-foot graphite, but occasionally, when splashed with nostalgia, I'll fish a delicate 7-foot, 3-weight cane rod balanced by an elderly Hardy Featherweight. The whole outfit puts a soft polish to my clumsy, sunrise attempts to deceive handsome trout with tiny flies.

Near Kellogg Bridge on North Down River Road, the river spreads and contracts, varying from about 70 to nearly 100 feet in width. There are deep bend pools, lively riffles, enticing flats, swift runs, and a few deep holes to shelter the trout. With prolific hatches and easy access, this may be the most heavily fished section of the North Branch.

Big Creek (south flowing) crosses North Down River Road just east of Kellogg's Bridge, enters the North Branch a short distance beyond, and adds significant, noticeable volume to the flow. The current feels heavier, there are deeper pockets, and the number of dark runs and holes increases. The fish are heavier as well and this is the most likely run in which to raise a trophy fish on the North Branch.

At first and last light, during overcast periods, and in the dead of night, a Woolly Bugger, a Houghton Lake Special, or a large sculpin pattern will frequently move large browns. A Deer-hair Mouse, or a night moth on a number 2 hook are productive surface alternatives. Brown trout like these big protein cartons—wet or dry.

Morley Road dead-ends at the river about one third of the distance between North Down River Road and the junction with the main stream. This is the last *convenient* public access.

The North Branch curves into a high-bank just a few yards downstream from the dead-end. The bottom is a mix of sand, gravel, some cobble, and clay patches with silt at the edges.

The current has power to it and pushes food and oxygen into the depths. This is brown drake habitat. As the river nears the mainstream, the fine gravel and sand continues, and more and more silt builds up along the edges and on the bottom of slow pools. Now we have a joyous mix of brown drakes, Hex, and *Isonychia* to tempt the biggest fish and quietly madden the angler.

June is the magic month on the North Branch. A guided trip in a classic Au Sable riverboat is a clear water float through history. There will be a warm breeze and high anticipation. There will be big bugs dancing and lusting through the shadows. Your guide will stop the boat with his push pole and stare at the current seam below an ancient sweeper. The water will bulge and he will say, "There. Are you ready?" You will be ready.

## The Big Water
## McMasters to Mio

This section of the Au Sable marks yet another transformation with the input of significant flows from the North Branch and from Big Creek. The transition from the small, comfortable stream at the upper end of the "flies-only" water near Grayling to the full-blown river at Mio is significant. At the gauging station in Grayling the mean annual flow averages 76.3 cubic feet per second; at Mio the mean annual flow averages 998 cfs, an impressive development of growth in less than 50 river miles.

From McMasters Bridge to the confluence with the North Branch of the Au Sable (approximately three miles) the river's run is predominantly pool and riffle. The North Branch introduces significant sedimentation and that impact, along with a more moderate gradient, produces a flat, smooth run with only occasional riffles downstream to Parmalee Bridge.

Although noticeably wider and deeper, the reach from the North Branch to Parmalee is reminiscent of the area near Connor's Flat. Its bottom is a mix of sand, fine gravel, some cobble, and silt. And the silt build up is noticeable. Again, this

◆

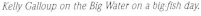

*Kelly Galloup on the Big Water on a big-fish day.*

*Big Creek in March—a vital tributary.*

◆

is prime *Hexagenia limbata* water and it is ardently courted by many during June and early July.

This stretch also presents angling opportunities with other hatches. Caddis and stoneflies are present and there are reasonable hatches of Hendricksons, sulphurs, and brown drakes. *Isonychias* (variously called white-gloved howdy, maroon drake, lead-winged coachmen, large mahogany drake) begin to show about mid-way through the Hex hatch and will last through July. This is a substantial bug and the trout look for them, particularly the spinners. The duns emerge sporadically throughout the day, but the spinner fall is concentrated at dusk. Look for *Isonychia* activity near riffles. Often the fish will queue in the smoothing transition water below a riffle and feed heavily into the darkness. As the Hex hatch wanes in early July, it is common enough (and very frustrating) to discover different fish in the same pool feeding selectively on either of the two spinners.

Below Parmalee Bridge, the river alternates between handsome pool and riffle sections and less attractive, but still productive, smooth, even runs until it meets the impoundment pond behind the dam at Mio. The river bottom varies from a sand and gravel mix to clay, muck, and silt in the slower flows. The deep runs and black holes at the bends harbor some of the largest browns in the river system.

The series of riffles, pools, and deep holes between Parmalee and the Luzerne park hold eager brookies and rainbows as well as brown trout. Forage fish include dace, darters, shiners, and sculpins, and the Muddler patterns do some of their best work in this stretch.

On a cloudy day in late May of 1996, gifted writer, Jerry Dennis and fly shop owner, Kelly Galloup joined me on a float from Parmalee Bridge to the Whirlpool access on Cherry Creek Road. Air temperatures were in the mid-fifties and the water varied from 49 to 52 degrees F. Both men are accomplished fly anglers and Kelly's reputation, fairly earned, is that of a big fish/streamer specialist.

The Hendrickson hatch had condensed and finished due to an abnormally warm 10-day period, and a series of moderate rains had added a light tinge to the usually clear water. We elected to fish streamers on sinking lines until circumstances, such as surface-feeding activity, dictated a change.

Kelly tied on a four-foot leader ending in 10-pound-test Maxima. To this, he added a strange looking sculpin pattern with a double wing of mallard flank feathers tied flat over the body. Jerry started with a Woolly Bugger and I rowed. I watched Kelly cast from the bow and followed the yellowish tan fly as it jerked and paused and fluttered on the retrieve. A hard, foot-long pull caused the fly to dart erratically and it fluttered and seemed to struggle for equilibrium on the pause.

Jerry and Kelly dropped their flies tight to the banks, close to stumps, and under the over-hanging trees. They mended, paused, stripped hard and paused again. We rounded a wide, bending riffle and dropped into a right-hand curve on the north bank. Kelly dropped the Zoo Cougar an inch from the grassy undercut and stripped hard, paused, then started the second strip when a large, yellowish form showed and the rod tip jerked violently. "Gone. I missed him." Five minutes later there was a repeat assault. This one came from under a leaning cedar and I thought I saw the trout come down on the fly from the top. It was another large fish and again it escaped

closer inspection. The day continued in this vein. We counted an even dozen fish in the 20-inch range that tried to eat the strange, fluttering sculpin. One fish was significantly larger. It hit about three feet from the drift boat and the rod doubled. Kelly said "ugh" and powered back with a strike that would cross a tarpon's eyes. The big brown returned the pull with its own energy and the line went slack. The fly was gone. "Bad knot?" I asked. "Big fish," Kelly answered. And we actually hooked, played, and touched a few as a bonus. It was a great day, indicative of the numbers of trophy fish in this stretch of the Au Sable.

From Parmalee, past Luzerne park and the Whirlpool, to the backwaters of Mio Pond, the fish habitat and the food forms are rich and varied. The lively riffles and deeper runs have mixed bottoms of sand, gravel, and cobble. The banks are undercut and lush with vegetation. There are silted edges and deep muck in the slow corners. Prolific hatches of Hendricksons, sulphurs, brown drakes, *Isonychia*, *Hexagenia limbata*, various caddis and stoneflies (including the giant *dorsata*) mix with dense sculpin and crayfish populations to provide substantial fodder for trout.

This is one of my favorite sections of the Au Sable. It presents varied water types and scenery along with reliable hatches and the knowledge that any cast may produce an encounter with a true trophy by any standard of measurement. If a friend wants to find and touch a 20-inch or better brown trout, this is one of the three sections of the system that we will float. We will see mink, muskrats, raccoons, and deer. Kingfishers will scold, herons will stalk, we might see an eagle. Dusk settles and we wait. The Hex spinners come and the greedy feeding sounds out there in the dark mix with a coyote chorus.

◆

*A "hot" run for big fish upstream from Mio.*

*Crayfish and sculpin produce very large trout in this reach of the river.*

## Mio to Alcona

At the foot of Mio Dam, visible from highway M-33, the river churns large, dark, and ominous. As it spreads through the riffles below the highway, banks past the boat launch, and curves away into the Huron National Forest, the visual impact is more inviting. The water is clear, the streambed is wide with a visible gravel and rock bottom that shows a golden hue in the morning sun. Although it is still more than 90 river-miles to Lake Huron, only 42 miles can be classified as a flowing river. The impoundments behind the five downstream dams claim the remainder.

The stretch from Mio to Alcona covers close to 30 miles of near wilderness. From Mio to Comins Flats, approximately seven miles, there are only three locations with cabins or homes. From Comins Flats to McKinley, about eight miles, cabins are more numerous but are clustered into compact stretches. The downstream run from McKinley to the access at Forest Service Road 4001 has no structures of any kind, and the short flow from 4001 to the impoundment behind Alcona Dam perpetuates the bucolic experience.

The beautiful and enduring reach from Mio to Alcona seems out of place in the upper Midwest. It is of a size, character, and aura that is more suggestive of a western environment. And it is relatively unknown, an under-appreciated mystery to the region's fly anglers despite its prolific, reliable hatches and trophy-sized fish. This is a big river, more clearly dangerous than the inviting Holy Water, and much less publicized.

Just below the boat launch at Mio a powerline crosses the river. From that point to McKinley Bridge, a distance of 15-plus miles, special "trophy" regulations are in effect. Only artificial lures may be used and both the size and "keep" restrictions were implemented to stimulate the development of trophy-sized trout.

*The uppermost dam at Mio, Michigan.*

*Kevin and Joe with a 26-inch "friend" on a cool September day.*

The first four miles below Mio is a run of alternating pools and riffles with a sand, gravel, and cobble bottom. This run has dense caddis and stonefly populations, excellent hatches of Hendricksons, sulphurs, brown drakes, *Isonychia*, some March browns, various olives, and the white fly (*Ephoron luekon*). The ever-present crayfish and sculpin represent bulk protein to the larger trout, and during non-hatch periods, are a suggested alternative to small, wet fly patterns.

From the downstream edge of the Loop Campground it is about four miles to Comins Flat. The river spreads and smooths in this reach, but there remain sufficient riffles to maintain the desirable mix of mayflies, caddis, and stoneflies.

At Perry Creek Flat, the Au Sable is long and broad and safely wadeable with just an ounce or two of common sense. The bottom here is firm and the flow consistent and moderate. A thoughtful angler will approach cautiously from the north bank and closely watch for feeding fish. The far bank (south side) is deeper and provides more cover and shade. Not surprisingly, this is the section that holds the most trout. But the fish move throughout the flat and often take up feeding stations in mid-channel or in shallow water near the north bank below the entrance of Perry Creek. Wade carefully and be patient. My biggest fish from Perry Creek Flat was a 23-inch brown that ate a size 14 Adams during a Hendrickson hatch. She was feeding on the north bank in less than a foot of water.

Looking downstream from the flat, you will see a long, river-wide riffle. Below the riffle, the river flattens into a large pool that bends to the left and out of sight. The riffle is home to both browns and rainbows and is easy to fish from the north side. In the evening, larger fish congregate at the head of the pool to feed. Both the brown drake and white fly hatches provide excitement in this location.

As the river curves left it passes through the meadows area, back into a series of riffles and pools, past high sand banks with deep holes, and into a series of curves before the long, straight run above Comins Flats. All of this is home to picky, seemingly moody brown trout of significant proportion. The brown drake hatch is your best opportunity to hook one on a dry fly. Large stonefly patterns cast into the midnight ink also produce along with the *Isonychia* and white fly. But the majority of the very large fish are caught on big streamers and a high percentage of those are hooked on dark sculpin patterns on size 2 and 4 hooks. I saw many fish over 25 inches released in this stretch in 1996. Two ate olive Zoo Cougars and one munched a classic Muddler.

The water at Comins Flats is broad, relatively shallow, and easily waded. It is open, inviting, and an excellent spot for a newcomer (to the sport or to the river) to get a feel for casting and wading in big water. Immediately upstream from the launch ramp, the river is split by an island. The convergence of currents at the island, the south-side bank, the deep riffles below the ramp, and the sweeping pool at the left-hand curve all hold rainbows and browns—some quite large.

The run from Comins to McKinley moves from a pool/riffle habitat to one dominated by a flat, smooth run with a sand

*September 30, 1997, the last fish of the last day.*

bottom punctuated with a few deep riffles that offer gravel and some cobble. Larger trout shelter in deep curves near high banks and in the back eddies behind structure. The banks and slower pools show a build-up of silt, and as the river nears McKinley, suitable habitat for the *Hexagenia limbata* increases.

The public access at Davis Landing offers a happy combination that includes safe wading, good hatches and sizable trout in a variety of water types. Upstream from the parking area a long, broad run curves into a deep channel that spreads through a wide riffle into a flat, productive pool. There are large fish throughout, and the Hendricksons, brown drakes, and *leukons* bring them to the surface.

The Bear Hole, also known as Coyote Bluff, is easily reached from McKinley Road—about 1.5 miles upstream from the village of McKinley. This spot offers a variety of water types including a long, sweeping pool on the upstream side, a smooth flat edge with a deep, heavy riffle directly across, and on the downstream side, a bending, right-hand curve that blends into a silted, deep hole. A few Hex show in this part of the river and they often overlap with both brown drakes and *Isonychia*. The best fishing here is during the late evening hours through the month of June. Be ready for spinner falls of sulphurs (size 18, 20) preceding brown drakes (size 8, 10) and *Isonychia* (10, 12). Carry a few Hex spinners (6) and perhaps a clipped Deer-hair Mouse on a size 2 hook.

The bridge over the river at McKinley marks the downstream boundary of the special regulation "trophy" water, but not the end of prime trout angling. Below the bridge there is a run of mostly flat water for about two miles. A few riffles break up the regularity of the smooth flow and hold both rainbow and brown trout. After the flat run, the river moves into a reach with numerous riffle and pool sequences and heavy shading along the deep, often grassy banks. There are no cabins, no man-made structures here. This is a wild river.

White and Norway pines, oaks, cedars, poplar, beech,

*Weekend canoers at the Mio launch*

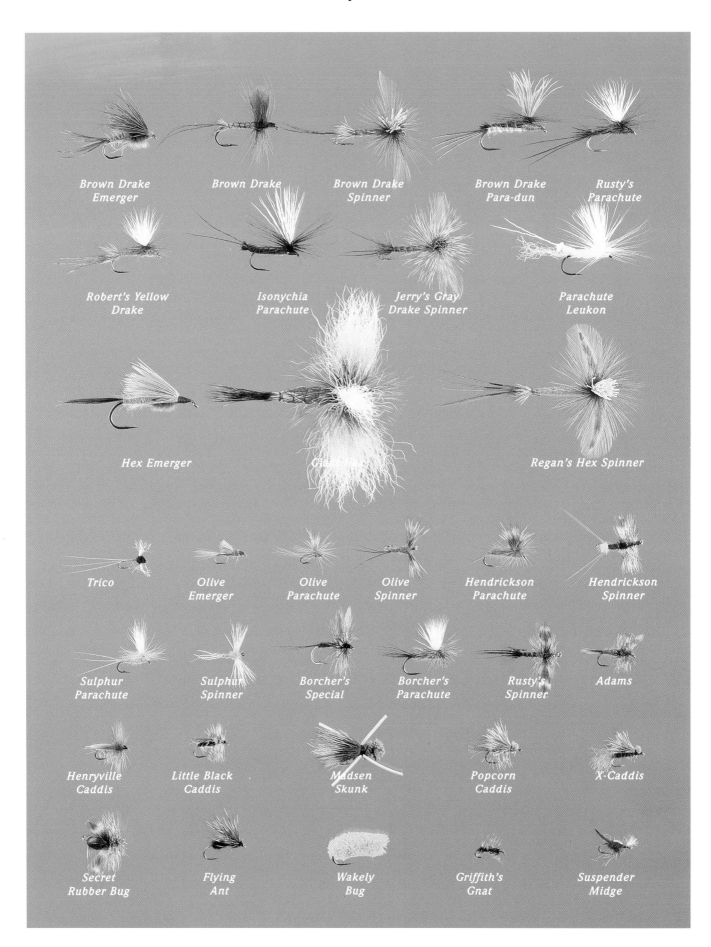

Brown Drake
Emerger

Brown Drake

Brown Drake
Spinner

Brown Drake
Para-dun

Rusty's
Parachute

Robert's Yellow
Drake

Isonychia
Parachute

Jerry's Gray
Drake Spinner

Parachute
Leukon

Hex Emerger

Regan's Hex Spinner

Trico

Olive
Emerger

Olive
Parachute

Olive
Spinner

Hendrickson
Parachute

Hendrickson
Spinner

Sulphur
Parachute

Sulphur
Spinner

Borcher's
Special

Borcher's
Parachute

Rusty's
Spinner

Adams

Henryville
Caddis

Little Black
Caddis

Madsen
Skunk

Popcorn
Caddis

X-Caddis

Secret
Rubber Bug

Flying
Ant

Wakely
Bug

Griffith's
Gnat

Suspender
Midge

Jerry's Hopper

Giant Stonefly

Earl Madsen's Gray Stonefly

Yellow-Bellied Mattress Thrasher

Brown Drake Nymph

Hex Nymph

Squirrel Nymph

Olive Nymph

Pheasant Tail Nymph

Hare's Ear Nymph

Tellico

Puff Nymph

Cased Caddis

Tan Soft Hackle

Warbird

Houghton Lake Special

Zonker

Earl Madsen Buzz Saw

Olive Clouser

Olive Blaster

Woolly Sculpin

Zoo Cougar

Rock's Crayfish

Deer Hair Mouse

*Tequila Sunrise*     *Popsicle*

*Black Stone Fly*     *Latex Wiggler*     *Hare's Ear*     *Bead-butt Hare's Ear*

*Green Caddis*     *Au Sable P.T.*     *Philoplume Hex*     *Sparrow Nymph*

*Chartreuse Wiggler*     *Egg Sucking Leech*     *Micro Egg*     *Egg Fly*     *Egg Fly*

hickory, and hemlock blend with wild iris, goldenrod, violets, fairy slippers, grasses, sedges, and moss. Eagles threaten ospreys, red-tailed hawks, gulls, and terns. Deer, black bears, and coyotes drink in the shallows. Mink, otter, beaver, perhaps even a marten, patrol the banks. And in the cooling dusk, nighthawks and bats circle and dart through the pulsing clouds of mayflies.

There is much more silt here and, correspondingly, a build-up of the *Hexagenia limbata* population. From about June 12th through the end of the month the bugs emerge and mature sexually. About June 14th the spinners leave the trees in sufficient numbers to produce the desired reaction—a surface gorge by large brown trout.

About half-way between McKinley and 4001, and fairly close to Bear Island, there is a slight but noticeable narrowing of the river as it forms a deep chute and breaks into a hard, right turn. Just below this right-hand curve the bank is shallow

and wadeable while the center run remains deep and heavy. At the tail-out of the run the current slows again and bleeds into a wide, slow, glass-surfaced pool.

I have compared notes with friend and guide Kelly Neuman and our findings are consistent. Every time we have stopped our boats here a trophy fish has at least been hooked if not landed and released. Brown drakes, *Isonychia*, and the white fly jump-start the surface feeding, but the Hex is king. Browns over 20 inches are no surprise. A "24" or better is a fair expectation, and we lost one last year (Maxima 8-pound-test tippet) that would not be slowed or turned, let alone touched.

A Michigan native recently said to me, "This looks like the Snake or Big Horn. I didn't even know this was here. I've fished the upper river all my life and never seen this—but I'll be back." Miles Chance, who owns M. Chance Fly Fishing Specialties in Okemos, Michigan was more succinct. As he

## Significant Au Sable River Hatches

| Common Name | Scientific Name | Emergence | Hook Size |
|---|---|---|---|
| Blue-winged Olive | *Baetis vagans* | Late April-August | 18-20 |
| Slate-winged Mahogany Drake | *Paraleptophlebia adoptiva* | April 20-June 1 | 16 |
| Little Black Caddis | *Chimarra atterrima* | April 20-June 1 | 16-18 |
| *Dark Hendrickson | *Ephemerella subvaria* | May 1-20 | 14 |
| Hendrickson | *Ephemerella rotunda* | May 10-June 5 | 14 |
| Light Hendrickson Sulphur | *Ephemerella invaria* | May 10-May 30 | 16 |
| Borcher's Drake | *Leptophlebia nebulosa* | May 20-June 5 | 12-14 |
| Giant Black Stonefly | *Pteronarcys dorsata* | June-July 4 | 2-4 |
| Popcorn Caddis | *Nectopsyche* | June-August | 14-16 |
| Sulphur | *Ephemerella dorothea* | May 30-June 30 | 18-20 |
| *Brown Drake | *Ephemera simulans* | June 3-15 | 10 |
| Green Oak Worm | | June | 10-12 |
| Flying Ant | | June-August | 14-16 |
| *Giant Michigan Mayfly | *Hexagenia limbata* | June 12-July 8 | 6 |
| *Maroon Dun Gloved Howdy | *Isonychia sadleri/bicolor* | June 15-August | 10-12 |
| March Brown | *Stenonema vicarium* | June | 10-12 |
| Light Cahill | *Stenacron canadense* | June 20-July 20 | 12-14 |
| Slate-winged Olive | *Ephemerella lata* | June 25-August 20 | 16 |
| Tiny Olive | *Pseudocloeon anoka* | July-August | 24 |
| Trico/Tiny White-winged Black Quill | *Tricorythodes stygiatus* | August-September | 24-26 |
| *White Fly | *Ephoron leukon* | August 18-September | 12-14 |
| Grasshoppers | | August-September | 8-12 |
| Crickets | | August-September | 8-12 |

*Denotes hatches that reliably raise the largest fish.

◆

*The wide flats below McKinley require perfect drifts.*

*Now-retired district fisheries biologist Dave Smith checks oxygen in late winter.*

◆

revived a 24-inch female brown at two in the morning. He looked skyward and said, "This is great. Thank you."

## The Big Water
## Alcona to Foote

The backwaters behind Alcona Dam cover 1,075 surface acres. Below the surface the original streambed's hydraulic gradient drops as much as 10.53 feet per mile. Some of the richest trout habitat in the entire system is now a lake. This impoundment is managed as a warm-water fishery with stocked populations of walleye, northern pike, smallmouth and largemouth bass. In addition to the game fish, all of the impoundments support suckers, carp, bowfin, and bullheads.

The flow from Alcona Dam to the impoundment behind Loud Dam is the last stretch of true river until the Au Sable is discharged from Foote Dam and proceeds on its final meander to Lake Huron. But, although the water has been warmed by Alcona Pond, it is not to be discounted as a fly-fishing venue.

From the public access immediately below Alcona on Bamfield Road, the river flows nearly due south through a continuum of sweeping curves and tight bends interspersed with frequent pool and riffle combinations. The bottom is mixed sand, gravel, cobble, clay, and silt. Access is extremely limited in this wild run through the national forest.

The first few miles of river provide fast and consistent fly rod action with chunky and aggressive smallmouth bass. They lie in ambush near the sunken logs, under the shade of over-hanging trees, near the larger mid-riffle rocks, and in the deep pools.

This is high sport. A short float of three or four miles will usually produce at least a dozen bass between 12 and 18 inches. These fish really thump the fly on the strike, then leap and churn and execute all of the special moves that make small-mouth such a highly prized fly-rod quarry. There are no

plodding palookas in this river. These are rock-hard sluggers that absolutely love light olive Muddlers, Yuk Bugs, black Woolly Buggers, and strip leech patterns. As the river continues south it is cooled by ground springs and tributaries. Near King's Corner Road, Hoppy Creek joins the Au Sable and this area has a respectable population of both brown and rainbow trout, some of which achieve formidable proportions. Brown drakes, Hex, and the white fly, lure the largest trout to the surface during spinner falls, and it is probable that one or two will show behind a streamer intended for smallmouth.

In mid-July of 1996 Kelly Neuman and I alternated casting and rowing on a float for bass. It was a warm, muggy morning and the smallmouth were eager. We used sink-tip lines, short leaders, and big flies. The fish were concentrated in the holes, deeper pools, and in the oxygenated riffles.

On our final rotation before the take-out, we approached a broad riffle that spread from the north bank to mid-river. A small spring fed in from a shaded hillside and I cast the fake sculpin into the current. I do not remember mending and I do not recall stripping line, but I do remember a solid strike followed by a very strong surge and a rapidly disappearing fly line. We both saw a long (mid-twenties?) silver fish with a broad pink band from cheek to tail. "Good Lord," said Kelly. "@*!#," said Bob, "he's gone." The fly slipped out somehow and the line curved through the current and straightened. Since dams block all upstream movement by potamodromous fish, this was a resident rainbow of steelhead proportion. So it goes.

Following Hoppy Creek, Stewart Creek and the South Branch River enter the mainstream before its inevitable spread into the backwaters of the impoundment behind Loud Dam.

There are still trout in this lower reach, but there are many more smallmouth, and the deep holes are refuge to walleyes and ravaging northern pike. I've never been much of a fan of either species although a walleye is great table fare, and the older boys tell me that northerns are an honorable and notable fly-rod adversary.

Due primarily to limited access, this part of the river is largely unexplored by fly anglers. One has to be a committed and healthy hiker, or be willing to spend considerable time and energy in boat or canoe to investigate the possibilities. But the scenery is worth every ounce of energy even if the fish are not responsive. There are high, dominating hills with a lush mix of hardwoods, conifers, grasses, and wild flowers. Crystal springs gurgle over rocks and through clay and sand to the river. The deep, inky bends are mysterious. What lies down there on the bottom? Perhaps a huge brown trout, perhaps a sturgeon, maybe Jimmy Hoffa. Perhaps the eagle and the otter know.

The water slows and backs up to form the pond behind Loud Dam near the Rollaway scenic overlook on Rollaway Road in western Iosco County. Highway 65 parallels the impoundment eastward, then turns north to cross the Au Sable at Five Channels. River Road continues due east, parallel with the impoundments behind Cooke and Foote dams. Approximately 20 percent of the entire mainstream lies

*Drift boat anchored not far from Perry Creek Flat.*

*Boston angler extraordinaire, Steve Pensinger, with a trophy smallmouth.*

◆

submerged from Loud to Foote. This was high gradient, first-quality recreational river. Now it is a lake, plodding its warmed water toward the final flow to Huron.

The ponds do provide recreational value however. Camping, boating, and angling for warm-water species are popular pastimes from ice-out through late fall. Both species of bass, northern, walleye, panfish, and musky are the primary backwater targets. The Canoer's Memorial, Lumberman's Monument, the Iargo Spring (a natural wonder 17 miles west of Oscoda) various scenic overlooks, and the *Au Sable Queen*, a sternwheel paddleboat, attract and entertain thousands of tourists yearly.

## Steelhead Water
## Foote Dam to Lake Huron

The volume of discharge at Foote Dam is 1,485 cfs compared with 998 at the Mio gauge station and 76.3 at Grayling. The river is only a few miles from Lake Huron at this point and has drained 1,932 square miles of watershed.

The 12-mile flow to the lake is mostly a smooth run through a series of bends, oxbows, and tight curves. The riffle/pool sections are less frequently encountered than in the upstream reaches, but because of their prime spawning gravel, they attract and concentrate large numbers of steelhead and salmon. The remainder of the river's bottom is dominated by sand with small, isolated gravel pockets that also lure fish and hold them in close proximity.

Although there is some limited walk-in access, this section of the Au Sable is best fished from a drift boat. The river is deep and clear with a constant, heavy flow that can quickly tire a wading angler. The water's clarity misleads the perception of depth, and the tangled deadfalls and remnant logs from the lumber drives are formidable hazards. There are, of course, several spots that afford comfortable wading, but few of these

◆

*A solitary reach in late September.*

*Steve Nevala takes a ride on the Big Water.*

♦

locations are within a comfortable hike from anywhere.

This section of river should be considered in two parts. The upper reach begins below the dam, off Rea Road, and extends to the Whirlpool access off River Road. There is a boat launch ramp and a large parking lot and toilet facility at the Rea Road Bridge just a few hundred yards downstream from the dam. These accommodations are repeated at the Whirlpool. This stretch covers about five river-miles and presents the best spawning and holding water in and near the riffles and isolated pockets of gravel. The lower reach begins at the Whirlpool and terminates in the town of Oscoda. The river spreads and slows, and there is less gravel than in the upstream run. Fish are most often found in the deep, slow water at the bends or in channels near the bank. This is a staging area for fish on their way to, or back from gravel, and a holding area for waiting out particularly cold water.

Steelhead can be found in the Au Sable every month of the year. Sporadic surges of summer-run fish can show (briefly) from late June through August, but this is a hit or miss game with long odds. The fall fish begin to trickle in behind the run of spawning salmon in early September. This run accelerates through October with aggressive steelhead determined to gorge on salmon eggs. The winter and spring fishery peaks in

late April and often continues through late May.

An Au Sable steelhead is a high-energy package, a direct descendent of the first steelhead planted in the Great Lakes

♦

*Pounding big streamers near Bear Island.*

*The Au Sable is the "river of sand" and the sand filters and purifies.*

*Author holds a typical October steelhead.*

◆

basin. Dan Fitzhugh, of Bay City, Michigan, made the region's first planting of rainbow trout in the Au Sable River in 1876. The fry were hatched from eggs from a migratory strain of fish brought to Michigan from the McCloud River in California. They adapted very well. Thank you, Dan.

Perhaps it is due to relatively light fly-fishing pressure, but the Au Sable steelhead are less finicky than their cousins on the west side of the state. They are eager consumers, occasionally downright aggressive, and are (in my opinion) the most powerful and electric of all the Great Lakes strains.

The "spring run" draws the most attention. Traditionally the action starts to pick up in mid-March, growing day by day through April when the water finally warms enough to excite the hens and move them to the gravel. Territorial bucks will chase streamers (particularly sculpin patterns), Strip Leeches, and Woolly Buggers. They will eat small egg patterns as well but seem to prefer nymphs. The hens are even more attuned to nymphs, especially fluttering Hex patterns and sparrow nymphs. The hens should be left alone while on the gravel, but they can be push-overs for a dead-drift through the dark pocket water. These fish will run from six pounds up. A big steelhead is anything over 12 pounds and a fair average is about eight.

Rick Kustich, guide and owner of the Oak Orchard Fly Shop in Albion, NY, joined Kelly Neuman and me on the last day of April, 1996. It had rained all night and Rick was fearful that the river would be high and dirty. But the Au Sable runs through a massive sand filter for its entire course. It had raised slightly and carried just a hint of color. The sky was a rolling mass of varying shades—all gray. The bulging clouds were pushed hard by gusts from Lake Huron and spit bursts of stinging rain. Most people stayed home. Only two other drift boats and a handful of walk-ins showed on our float from Rea Road to the Whirlpool. The air temperature was 42 and the stream thermometer read 47 degrees Fahrenheit. It was dead-solid perfect.

Rick is an expert fly angler, Kelly is the premier fly fishing guide on the lower river, and I have been at this game for over 40 years, so despite my bumbling, we had a benchmark day. We hooked and played too many steelhead (well over 20) and landed an extravagant percentage. They ate Hex nymphs, Green Caddis, Pheasant Tails, and Hare's Ears. They ran fast and jumped high. It was too much. When you get to the point that blurs memory and appreciation of each individual fish, it is past the time to quit. We agreed to leave them in peace. We reeled in and floated the last two miles without casting.

To my way of thinking, the fall run produces the most

*Department of Natural Resources team checking nets for radio-tagged fish on the frozen backwaters.*

pleasant and exciting fishing to be had anywhere. The steelhead ascend the river with a prime objective and that is to feed heavily on salmon eggs.

The weather is generally more stable in the fall. The nights are cool to cold and the days feature crisp mornings and warm afternoons through October. Maples flame orange and red on the hillsides blending with the yellow leaves of poplar, the more somber golden hues of oak, and ultimately to the steady greens of white pine and bank-side cedars. The river is low and clear. Thousands of king salmon crowd and chase across the redds. And behind the redds in the dark pockets, *mykiss* holds expectantly.

This is the time to fish egg patterns; double micro-eggs on stout #10 hooks and small Glo Bugs in Oregon cheese and fluorescent chartreuse are good bets. A dropper, or tandem rig that presents two colors, is an effective way to fish, but the Au Sable's submerged lumber will take a heavy toll. It is quite possible to lose as many as fifty flies through the course of a long day.

Spey patterns produce well during the fall. They are most effective cast across and allowed to swing through the holding water at depth. The smooth run below the lower Hairpin, the heavy riffle below the High Banks, and the flat run that centers the river at the Boy Scout camp are good locations to try traditional and marabou Speys on the upper section. Below

the Whirlpool, marabou patterns like Cook's Popsicle and Tequila Sunrise work best when pulsed through the deep holes or through the head of the run near Three Pipes.

As the salmon deteriorate and die in late October, the steelhead switch over to a nymph diet and drop into slower, deeper water. Try small Hex flies on size 10 hooks, Sparrow Nymphs in size 8, and 10, and slender-bodied black stonefly patterns in 10 and 12.

The king salmon that rush in from Lake Huron in September are not to be ignored. They reach weights in excess of 30 pounds and are a real stretch for an angler's endurance—even with heavy 9- and 10-weight rods.

The common misconception is that these fish will not take flies. But they do. Silver fish, fresh in from the lake, are very aggressive at first and last light. They will smash a wide range of large streamers from the gaudy Sarp's Seducer to the more subdued Zoo Cougar. The violent strike is, I think, triggered by territorial offensive rather than any urge to eat. Regardless of cause, the jolt is unforgettable. Once acclimated to the river, the salmon settle in on the business of procreation and seem to lose interest in streamers. However, they will continue to take nymphs fished on a clean, dead-drift. This is probably due to curiosity or minor annoyance, but the important fact is that the salmon take small flies right through their spawning period.

And the surroundings and atmosphere for salmon fishing

◆

*Durable hair-winged Speys.*

*"Magic time" near McMaster's.*

◆

have improved. Snagging is no longer legal in Michigan and it was first banned on the Au Sable, thanks largely to the selfless efforts of John Skrobot of Oscoda. John owns Calpyso Charters and guides anglers on Lake Huron and on the river. The ethical sporting public owes a great debt to John Skrobot. He lobbied hard, courageously, and successfully despite threats of physical violence from the dregs of society. Energetic law enforcement by the Iosco County Sheriff's Department and state conservation officers holds in balance the feral refuse that would continue to snag.

Deep winter at the end of my favorite river is magical. A friend and I will have it all to ourselves. We will share only with a solitary gull, perhaps a mink twitching and scurrying through the logs. The water will be very cold, near freezing. If the sun is shining and the air is cold enough, we will see water vapor crystallize and shoot into the air, then bend back toward us and the surface of the river. Tens of thousands of infinitesimal jewels weave a tenuous shine of light. It is called *diamond dust* and, on a beautiful river, is reward enough.

## Author's Parting Notes

The Anglers of the Au Sable is an organization dedicated to the environmental stewardship of the Au Sable watershed. The membership is committed to thoughtful, pro-active application of its resources to the aggressive protection of this beautiful river. For more information write to:

Anglers of the Au Sable
403 Black Bear Drive
Grayling, MI 49738

Special thanks to the Trout Unlimited chapters and Federation of Fly Fishers clubs that contribute directly with time, effort and dollars, to the specific care of the Au Sable. They include: Paul Young Chapter, Detroit; Challenge Chapter, Bloomfield Hills; George Mason Chapter, Grayling; Mershon Chapter, Saginaw; Martuch Chapter, Midland; Vanguard Chapter, Troy; and to the Flint Muddler Minnows FFF, the Red Cedar Fly Fishers FFF, and the North Branch Boys FFF.

## Fly Shops and Outfitters

### Upriver

**Gate's Au Sable Lodge**
417 Stephan Bridge Road
Grayling, MI 49738
(517) 348-8462

**Hartman's**
County Rd. 612
Lovells, MI 49738
(517) 348-9679

**The Fly Factory**
P.O. Box 709
Grayling, MI 49738
(517) 348-5844

### Downriver

**Streamside Rods & Guide Service**
7161 Trails End
South Branch, MI 48761
(517) 257-2499

**Nordic Sports**
218 West Bay St.
East Tawas, MI 48730
(517) 362-2001

**Bachelder Spool and Fly**
1434 East State St.
West Branch, MI 48661
(517) 345-8678

### Statewide

(These shops also track hatches and conditions on the Au Sable.)

**Troutsman**
4386 US 31 North
Traverse City, MI 49686
(800) 30 TROUT

**M. Chance Fly Fishing Specialties**
5100 Marsh Road
Okemos, MI 48864
(517) 349-6696

**The Benchmark**
32715 Grand River Ave.
Farmington, MI 48336
(810) 477-8116

**MacGregor's Outdoors**
803 N. Main
Ann Arbor, MI 48104
(313) 761-9200

**Paint Creek Outfitters**
203 E. University Drive
Rochester, MI 48307
(810) 650-0440

**Little Forks Outfitters**
143 East Main St.
Midland, MI 48640
(517) 832-4100

**Michigan Troutfitters**
3401 So. Huron
Bay City, MI 48706
(517) 684-3444

**Flymart**
1002 No. Main St.
Royal Oak, MI
(810) 584-2848

**Bueter's Outdoors**
120 E. Main St.
Northville, MI
(248) 349-3677

**The Riverbend Sport Shop**
29229 Northwestern Hwy.
Southfield, MI 48034
(248) 350-8484

---

### Camping Facilities Selected Sites

#### Upriver Area

North Higgins Lake State Park
South Branch, Roscommon
South Higgins Lake State Park
South Branch, Roscommon
Burton's Landing, Holy Water, Grayling
Keystone Landing, Holy Water, Grayling
Shupac Lake, North Branch, Lovells

#### Mid-river Area

Parmalee Bridge, Mainstream, Luzerne
Mio Pond, Mainstream, Mio
Wagner Lake, south of River, Mio

#### Downriver Area

Loop Campground, Trophy Water, Mio
Mack Lake, south of river, Mio
*River Dunes, Trophy Water, Mio
*Meadow Springs, Trophy Water, Mio

*Buttercup, Big Water, McKinley
Bear Island, Big Water, McKinley
Horseshoe Lake, northeast of river, Glennie
South Branch River, tributary, South Branch
Rollaways, Loud Dam Pond, South Branch
Monument, Cooke Dam, Oscoda

### Additional Camping Information

**State Parks** (517) 373-1270
**State Forest Campgrounds** (517) 373-1295
**Huron National Forest,** mid, (517) 826-3252
*non-motorized campgrounds; pack-in or boat access only

### Selected Points of Interest

**Kirtland Warbler;** Guided tours of nesting area of endangered songbird by USFS District Ranger Office Mio, (517) 826-3252

**Elk;** Pigeon River State Forest north of Grayling Wolverine, (517) 983-4101

**Civilian Conservation Corps Museum;** Exhibits outline the history of CCC established by Franklin Roosevelt, 1933. North Higgins Lake State Park, (517) 821-6125

**Lumbering Museum;** Hartwick Pines State Park; One of Michigan's last remaining stands of virgin white pine. Grayling, (517) 348-7068

**Our Lady of the Woods Shrine;** Large stone shrine in Mio on M-72.

**Lumberman's Monument;** Large statue and scenic overview of the Au Sable valley and Cooke Dam Pond on River Road, west of the town of Oscoda.

**Big Creek Perserve;** Private spring-fed trout lakes, fly-fishing-only, catch & release, upland birds, sporting clays. Mio, (517) 826-3606

### Fishing and Travel Information

**Michigan Department of Natural Resources,** Lansing
**Fisheries Division**
(517) 373-1280
**Law Enforcement**
(517) 373-1230
**Region II Headquarters, Roscommon,**
(517) 275-5151
**District 7 (Mio)**
(517) 826-3211

**Michigan Travel Bureau,** Lansing, (800) 543-2937
East Michigan Tourist Association, Bay City, (517) 895-8823
**Grayling Area Visitors Council,** (800) YES-8837
Oscoda County Council, (800) 800-6133

**Huron National Forest**
Mio Ranger District, (517) 826-3252